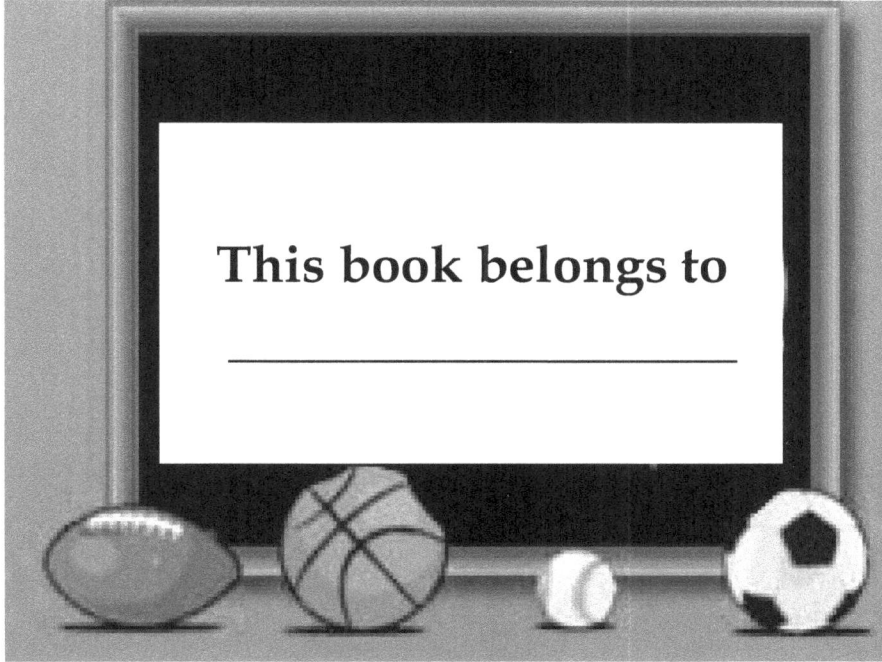

This book belongs to

_____

The Math Playbook Student's Activities

Let's Run Some Plays!

Teresa L. Batson, M.A.

Purposed4Success books are available at special discounts for bulk purchases and fundraisers in the U.S. by corporations, institutions, and other organizations. Please contact us at anointedconcepts3@gmail.com.

Written by Teresa L. Batson, M.A.

Graphics by David L. Gilkey, Timothy Ngiri, various artists at www.openclipart.org, and Teresa L. Batson

This book is a companion workbook to *The Math Playbook*. To purchase both books, go to www.themathplaybook.com.

The crossword puzzle was created on http://edtools.mankindforward.com.
The word search puzzles were created on http://www.word-search-world.griddler.co.uk.

This activities book is inspired by and dedicated to my fellow U.C.L.A. math study buddies, especially Rod from Cerritos, CA, who shared his amazing and thorough high school pre-calculus notes (math journal) with us in Calculus 31A and 31B.

ISBN 9780996232678

Printed in the United States of America

Purposed4Success Publishing
"We are all purposed for success." ~ Ruby Leah

TABLE OF CONTENTS

Welcome!

Thank you for investing in the companion workbook for *The Math Playbook* (the playbook). This workbook is designed to assist you in actively using the information and suggestions, also known as "the plays" discussed in the playbook. Let's enhance your mathmind, Student! Let's get your entire team set up for success on the field by reinforcing the fundamental building blocks for success in mathematics and other science-based subjects. As mentioned in the playbook, it is important for each member of your team to have an intention with the right mindset and a plan of action. This workbook is comprised of activities to help your teammates with those goals and more!

This workbook is organized in a way to be read by both coach and student. The pages are to be completed by both coach and student, as appropriate. Use the recommended resources, other resources you have on hand, or those that you acquire to "run the plays" covered in the following pages.

The activities parallel the chapters (the four quarters and half-time) in the playbook. There are four to seven sections per quarter in this workbook. The activities in a chapter/quarter can be completed over one week, two weeks, or a month. Coach, as suggested in the playbook, make sure to intentionally schedule time every week to have your student complete the activities in this workbook. Incorporate the activities in this workbook into your student's current math study routine. Consider setting up a 4-week, 8-week, or 12-week pace plan rotation. Then review, rinse, and repeat. **Browse through the entire book before getting started on the activities to determine which ones will best serve your team. Make sure to make duplicates of the activity pages before your student starts on the activities to have them available for future use.**

The majority of activities are designed to help you and your student set up and maintain your game plan. There are fun and games activities shared on these pages and links to access additional activities.

Equipment needed for activities in this workbook:
- Blank index cards
- Multiplication flashcards (or blank index cards)
- Pencils (for math problem-solving activities) and pens (for all other activities)
- Highlighters
- Journal or composition book, or binder with paper for journaling
- **Binder with paper to create an activity binder**

o Recording device (e.g., smartphone)

The expanded equipment inventory was discussed in the playbook and will be discussed in a later section.

Coach, schedule and monitor the activities regularly. Once you have identified your student's ideal study time, incorporate the activities in this workbook or schedule an additional 20 minutes to an hour a week to complete the activities included in this book. Check in with your student weekly to monitor progress. If you are the student, please find a team member to hold you accountable and to discuss the activities in the following pages with you.

Once your team completes all of the activities in this book, hold onto it and use the information your student has documented as a reference and a resource for lessons learned, future learning strategies, and memorialized achievements.

It is recommended that you have a workbook for each student on your team. Also, consider having all teammates work at the same pace to streamline the team's efforts and maximize resources.

For additional information and resources, please refer back to the playbook and go to www.themathplaybook.com.

THE 1st QUARTER PLAYS

"I never like to think about going back; I only look forward." ~ Alex Rodriguez

==

GET IN THE GAME!

The 1st Quarter sections are to be completed by the student. However, Coach, please assist where directed. Encourage your student to write in the workbook as opposed to them typing or having you dictate the information to them, unless an identified accommodation is needed. Make copies of these pages, as needed, for future use.

Student, considering that:

- Math is a language.

- Math is like a sport.

- Math concepts are important in everyday life.

- You will be learning and studying math throughout most of your academic journey.

Take 10 – 15 minutes to share below.

Date: _____

Today, what are you excited about? Your excitement can be about winning the game of math or something else.

_____

_____

_____

_____

_____

_____

_____

_____

_____

Share your concerns. What are the negative thoughts and self-talk you have about math up until now?

_____

_____

_____

==

_____
_____
_____
_____
_____
_____
_____
_____

What is your favorite sport up until now?

_____
_____
_____
_____
_____
_____
_____
_____
_____
_____

What is your favorite math concept up until now?

_____
_____
_____
_____
_____
_____
_____
_____
_____
_____

===

What are three things that you would like to do, learn, or achieve to improve your math game?

_____

_____

_____

_____

_____

_____

_____

_____

_____

_____

Based on the learning style descriptions discussed in the playbook on page 27, what is your primary learning style? What is your secondary learning style? Discuss with your coach or a teammate, if needed.

_____

_____

_____

_____

_____

_____

_____

_____

_____

_____

_____

Coach and Student, review these responses often. Update them every 12 – 24 weeks (90-180 days).

===

EQUIPMENT INVENTORY

Student, it's all in the setup! Let's set you up for success!

1. With your coach, review the list below and take inventory of the current equipment that you use to complete your mathematics class work and homework.
 2. Copy this list and check off items needed. Note that index cards/flashcards will be needed in an upcoming section.
3. Depending on the time in the school year, set a day and time to stock your equipment supply.

- o Vocabulary terms list
- o Flashcards
- o Lead pencils
- o Colored pencils
- o Pencil case
- o Highlighters
- o White erasers
- o Straight edge (e. g., a ruler)
- o Lined paper
- o Graph paper
- o Index cards
- o Binders
- o Math Journal/Playbook – A binder with loose leaf paper or a composition book is fine
- o Coins, macaroni, beans, chips, tiles, base 10 blocks, and other counting manipulatives
- o Squares, blocks and other shapes, and an abacus
- o Dice
- o Rulers, yardsticks, measuring tape – standard and metric
- o Right triangle
- o Protractor

- o Pencil sharpener
- o Calculators (the one in your student's brain; others are optional)
- o Mathematics book
- o Dictionary - college edition recommended
- o Thesaurus
- o Stapler or paper clips
- o Sticky Notes
- o Scratch paper*
- o Printer/Copier/Scanner
- o Three-hole punch
- o Clipboard
- o Measuring cups
- o Backpack or tote bag
- o Study center organizer
- o Tablet and Smart Phone Apps
- o Maps
- o Play Money
- o Differentiated instruction equipment – see the *Half-Time Report*
- o

REAL-LIFE PLAYS

Stay in the zone! Get in the zone! Math is everywhere! Over the next week or two, list three to five daily experiences or activities where you've seen math in action. Examples include shopping, cooking, watching a sporting event, and riding in a car. Write down the experiences and activities and how math was involved. Also, discuss your observations with your coach or teammates.

Date: _____

_____

_____

_____

Date: _____

_____

_____

_____

Date: _____

_____

_____

_____

Date: _____

_____

_____

_____

Date: _____

_____

_____

_____

WIN!

PRACTICE, CONDITIONING, & DRILLS

Student, please review the vocabulary list below and the multiplication facts list on an upcoming page. Talk with your coach to determine which one you want to tackle first – vocabulary terms or multiplication facts. These activities will be offered at another time in this workbook, too. Complete the associated enrichment activities as determined by you and your coach.

Let's review the vocabulary list from the playbook to set up the vocabulary mastery activities. The vocabulary terms are loosely grouped by math concept/building block. Select five to ten vocabulary terms and one to two multiplication facts sets to learn, understand, and/or memorize over the next 7 to 14 days using the Vocabulary Mastery Activities on the next page. If you don't see vocabulary terms that you need to master, use your math book or other resources to learn terms that you will be using in upcoming lessons or classes. The multiplication facts activities are covered in an upcoming page.

Use the study techniques on the following pages to guide your efforts. Ask your coach or a teammate to help you set up these activities if needed.

Arithmetic/Applied Arithmetic/Pre-Algebra Vocabulary

real number	absolute value	counting numbers	odd number
even number	prime number	composite number	whole number
number line	integer	positive number	negative number
rational number	irrational number	ascending order	descending order

****

| place value | ones | units | tens | hundreds-thousands |
| ten-thousands | digit | round | estimate | approximate(ly) |

****

| add | plus | together | sum | total | increase | addend |

****

| subtract | minus | takeaway | difference | fewer than | less than |
| decrease | reduce | reduction | deduction | | |

****

multiply times factor (n) product double

twice triple quadruple of exponent power order of operation

****

divide divisor dividend quotient factor (v) separate

into equal parts inverse operation reciprocal

****

decimal decimal point digit tenth

hundredth thousandth ten-thousandth

****

fraction numerator denominator improper fraction mixed number

reciprocal multiplicative inverse ratio proportion

****

percent part whole of is total

****

unknown variable constant order of operation

****

problem exercise Equation expression sentence

solve simplify calculate compute evaluate

equal equivalent same as average mean

median mode range greater than less than

greater than or equal less than or equal compare graph

****

linear one-dimensional two-dimensional three-dimensional

===

<u>Vocabulary Mastery Activities</u>

Coach and Student,

    Plan to dedicate 15 to 30 minutes to the activities 2 to 5 days a week for the next 7 to 14 days. Determine a convenient time where you can focus on completing the activities. Post those times on a calendar and/or planner. Use the weekly schedule in the playbook appendices.

Coach,

    On Day 1, you (or a teammate) can give your student a written assessment on 10 to 15 terms from the list at a time. Use your student's math book or other resources to obtain the definitions and applications of the math vocabulary, if needed. With the results of the assessment, assign your student 5 to 10 terms to study over a one-week to two-week span. Create a list of the terms on a piece of paper and post them on the refrigerator to view daily. Encourage family members to reference this list to help your student learn, understand, and apply the terms.

Student,

Commit to the 15 to 30 minutes time slot selected. Find a comfortable place to do these activities – comfortable seating and adequate lighting. Have snacks and study tools on hand. Turn on background music if it helps you focus.

DAY 0

1. Take the assessment. To the best of your ability, write the definition of each term **in your own words**.
2. Have your coach or another team member correct your answers.

DAY 1

    For any term that you don't know yet, write the term with the correct definition THREE times each in your math journal or a binder. Use your math textbook or go to www.mathsisfun.com/basic-math-definitions.html or other resources to get more understanding of these terms.

===

BONUS ACTIVITY – *Use a recording device to create an auditory fill-in-the-blank exercise to practice. Record yourself. First, state the definition of a term. Pause for three to five seconds. Then say the term. Leave the silent space between stating each definition and its correct term. Do this for each term on your list. **The silent space will allow time you to later say the term before the answer is revealed on the recording.** (This activity can be done outside of study time and is a great activity for auditory learners!)*

DAY 2

Create and use flashcards to study the terms.

DAY 3

Write the terms and definitions one to three times each.

DAY 4

1. Use the flashcards or the bonus activity to study/test yourself on the terms and definitions.
2. OR, define the terms and explain them to your coach or another team member. If you get 80% of the answers correct – CONGRATULATIONS!!!!!

DAY 5

Ask your coach or another team member to give you a written post-assessment. Afterward, take note of any incorrect answers and write those terms and definitions three times each. If you get 80% or more of the answers correct – CONGRATULATIONS!!!!!

Repeat this activity up to three times with new sets of five to ten words before moving on to The 2nd Quarter Plays activities. Coach, set up the next week's/section's practice set to include two or three of the terms from the previous week(s), especially those that your student hasn't mastered yet, for review and reinforcement. Just like the words "the", "read", and "yes" will come up in your student's conversations or reading material for years to come, the basic arithmetic terms will show up often in your student's math learning journey and life experiences.

===

Multiplications Facts Families

Student,

It is extremely important to learn the multiplication facts during or before 3rd grade to ensure future success in math classes. Fortunately, learning this set of numbers is a drill instead of a problem-solving exercise. If you do not know the complete set of facts for numbers 1 to 12, obtain or make flashcards, print out practice sheets from the resources mentioned below, and practice, practice, practice until they are learned. Use flashcards to have your coach or another study buddy drill you. Additionally, you may use a voice recorder to recite the multiplication facts in your voice to practice independently. This technique was explained in the playbook. By utilizing these enrichment exercises and any others that work for you, you can learn all of these facts in a few weeks. The sooner the sets of facts are learned, understood, and memorized, and you can give a correct answer/product verbally (or in writing) in less than three seconds, the better.

As mentioned in the playbook, I recommend that you study any fact sets you have not yet memorized in the order below. So, if you have already mastered facts 0 to 11, start with the 9 facts set. Then proceed to the 3 facts set. Use the practice sheets that are available on www.math-drils.com, www.math-aids.com, www.purplemath.com, or from other resources to which you have access to give yourself practice drills. Consult your coach or a teammate for any help with setting up this activity.

Study and memorize the facts in the order shown below. Please use this strategy and the tracking sheet on the next page to master the multiplication facts. Note that the 0 fact family results in a product of 0 based on the Zero Multiplication Property in each case. Zero multiplied by any value(s) equals zero; that's an easy score on the tracking sheet!

$$0, 1, 2, 5, 10, 11, 9, 3, 4, 6, 7, 8, 12$$

You might ask, "Why should I memorize the multiplication families in this order?" Through my experience with students on various grade levels, this order allows students to learn more information at a faster rate by using tips, tricks, and time-saving strategies like patterns that are more obvious in certain factor families. For example, the multiplication facts for the number nine (9) are easy to remember because the digits of the products add up to 9 – 9 x 3 = 27……. 2 + 7 = 9.

===

If you already know the facts sets for numbers 1 to 12, then learn the facts for 13-16, 20, and 25. These multiplication fact sets will often be referenced in algebra and geometry exercises. I refer to the multiplication operation as the "phonics of math." Mastering and memorizing these basic multiplication facts sets make blending math concepts easier in advanced courses.

Reminder: Create an activity binder or use your math journal/binder to store the activity sheets.

The Mathminded Multiplication Facts Tracking Sheet

Fact Set	Practice Date	Practice Date	Practice Date	Practice Date	Memorized Date
1					
2					
5					
10					
11					
9					
3					
4					
6					
7					
8					
12					
Expanded					
20					
25					
15					
13					
14					
16					
Advanced					
17					
18					
19					

===

FUN & GAMES –MATH MENTAL ENRICHMENT ACTIVITIES

Student, it is important to make learning fun! If you ever feel overwhelmed or lose focus when studying math concepts at home, call "Timeout!" Let your coach know you need to take a 15 to 30 minute mental break. Get some fresh air, take a power nap, turn on some music, move your body, create some art, have a snack, play a game, and/or engage in an enrichment activity. (Choose a game or activity that is not on television or another electronic device.☺)

On the next page, there is a crossword puzzle to solve when you need to take a break or want to test your math language skills. See the list of additional enrichment activities after the puzzle. Have fun!

===

BASIC MATH VOCABULARY FUN

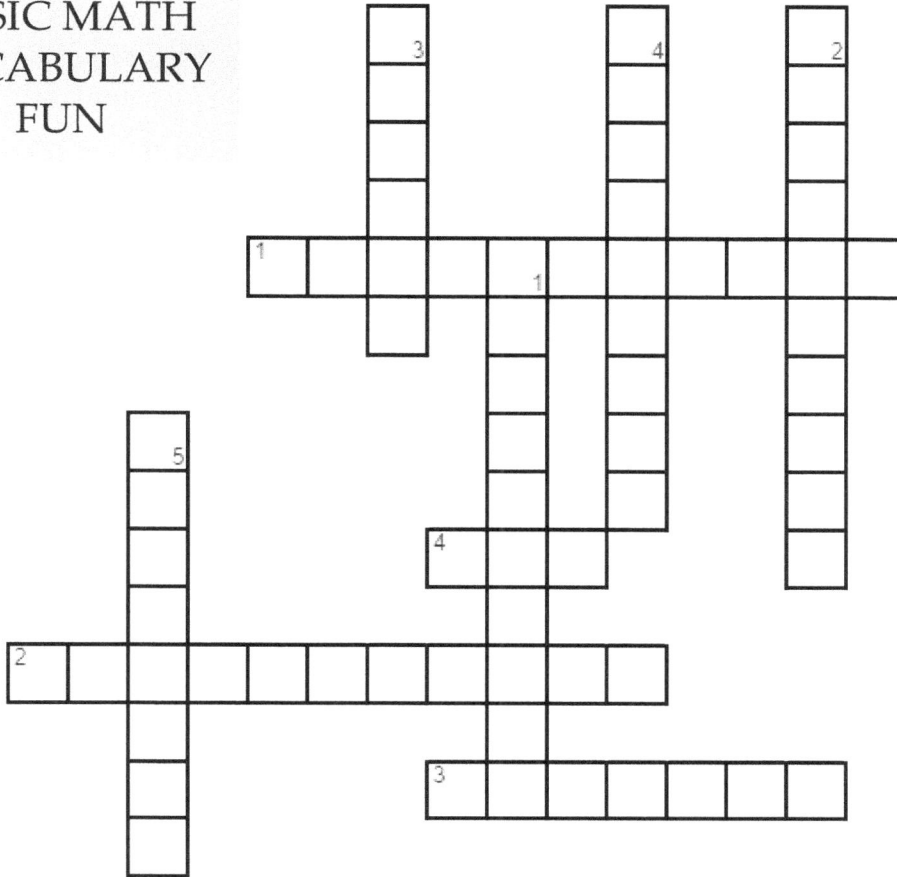

Across

1. a number without fractions or decimals
2. a number that only has two factors 1 and itself
3. the answer to a multiplication problem
4. the answer to an addition problem

Down

1. a number (integer) evenly divided by 2
2. the answer to a subtraction problem
3. numbers you multiply together to get another number
4. a number (integer) that can't be divided by 2
5. the answer to a division problem

For the answers, go to www.themathplaybook.com.

Additional Timeout Ideas & Resources

- Check out www.math-aids.com. Download three to five activities for future use.

- Explore your house or neighborhood. Use graph paper to create a floor plan or a map.

- Enjoy one of the following:

  - Jigsaw puzzle

  - Sudoku

  - Cooking

THE 1ST QUARTER PLAYS LESSONS LEARNED 👉☺

Student, list anything that you have realized or learned about yourself, your relationship to math, your current or past learning experiences, and/or your study strategies up until now. Discuss these lessons with your coach or another teammate and explore how you can improve the situations moving forward.

Date: _____

_____

_____

_____

_____

_____

_____

_____

_____

Date: _____

_____

_____

_____

_____

_____

_____

_____

_____

_____

Date: _____

_____

_____

_____

_____

_____

_____

_____

_____

THE 1ST QUARTER WINNING PLAYS 🏅

List three to five of your successes over the past one to four weeks! The successes could be in any area of your life. You can also list people, experiences, resources, and things for which you are grateful.

Date: _____

_____

_____

_____

_____

_____

_____

_____

Date: _____

_____

_____

_____

_____

_____

_____

_____

Date: _____

_____

_____

_____

_____

_____

_____

_____

THE 1ST QUARTER SIDELINE NOTES

Coach and Student, write down any next steps to take, adjustments to be made, and any other important information to consider.

Date: _____

_____
_____
_____
_____
_____
_____
_____
_____
_____
_____
_____
_____
_____
_____
_____
_____
_____
_____
_____
_____
_____
_____
_____
_____

THE 2nd QUARTER PLAYS

"Dedication makes dreams come true." ~ Kobe Bryant

YOUR WINNING TEAM 👪

Student, you should have invested a week, two weeks, or up to a month completing the activities in The 1st Quarter Plays. Well done! Now, let's make sure you have the teammates necessary to execute your game-winning plan. Please share any concerns and ideas with your coach regarding your teacher/instructor, classroom experience, a tutor, study buddies, and your study area. Also, write them below.

Date: _____

Current Grade/Math Subjects Experience

_____
_____
_____

Current Teacher(s)/Instructor(s)

_____
_____
_____

Current/Potential Tutor(s)

_____
_____
_____

Current/Potential Study Buddies

_____
_____
_____

Current/Potential Coach(es) – to collaborate with your coach

_____
_____
_____

Current/Potential Team and Study Song/Playlist

_____
_____
_____

THE PLAYING FIELD (STUDY AREA) SETUP

Student, if you already have a designated study area and study time, what would improve your study sessions, especially when you study math? If you don't already have a designated study area, consider where it could be set up and what items you will need to make it a good place for you to focus and thrive. Consider an alternative study area like the library, community center, or park, too. Also, consider the best times for you to study alone and with your teammates. Discuss the options with your coach.

Current or Ideal Study Area Location and Backup Location:

_____

_____

_____

Current or Ideal Study Sessions (days per week):

_____

_____

_____

Current or Ideal Study Time Duration (30 minutes to 90 minutes):

_____

_____

_____

Current or Ideal Study Time Snacks:

_____

_____

_____

Current or Ideal Study Buddy Sessions Days and Times:

_____

_____

_____

Study Area Items Needed (like better lighting and music; see the equipment/school supplies list on page 5):

_____

_____

_____

MAKE A COMMITMENT ✋

Student, have you and your coach read and signed the commitment sheets yet? If not, please do that after your coach completes reading The 2nd Quarter in the playbook. For now, answer the following questions about commitment.

What is a game, activity, project, or cause that you have been committed to until completion? What inspired you to stay with it? How did you feel once it was completed?

_____

_____

_____

_____

List three to five obstacles that have slowed down your learning, understanding, application, and/or mastery of math concepts in the past.

_____

_____

_____

_____

What are three to five actions you can take to stay committed even when more obstacles appear? Discuss this with your coach.

_____

_____

_____

_____

What are three easy short-term goals (over the next 30 days) that you are committed to achieving?

_____

_____

_____

_____

What are three ways in which you can make the above actions and attaining the goals easy and fun?

_____

_____

_____

_____

==

REAL-LIFE PLAYS

Stay in the zone! Math is everywhere! Over the next week or two, list three to five daily experiences or activities where you've seen math in action. Examples include shopping, cooking, watching a sporting event, and riding in a car. Write down the experiences and activities and how math was involved. Also, discuss your observations with your coach or teammates.

Date: _____

_____

_____

_____

Date: _____

_____

_____

_____

Date: _____

_____

_____

_____

Date: _____

_____

_____

_____

Date: _____

_____

_____

_____

WIN!

==

FUN & GAMES – MATH MENTAL ENRICHMENT ACTIVITIES

Student, it is important to make learning fun! If you ever feel overwhelmed or lose focus when studying math concepts at home, call "Timeout!" Let your coach know you need to take a 15 to 30 minute mental break. Get some fresh air, take a power nap, turn on some music, move your body, create some art, have a snack, play a game, and/or engage in an enrichment activity. (Choose a game or activity that is not on television or another electronic device.☺)

Here is a recipe to make when you need to take a break and have a healthy snack. Find a list of websites with additional enrichment activities on the next page. Have fun!

This salad recipe is a "go-to dish" for me that always gets rave reviews when I take it to potluck events! I saw the dish demonstrated at a grocery store, and I added the carrots, red pepper flakes, and pecans to kick it up a notch! It contains highly alkaline ingredients, which are great for the digestive and immune systems. So, you can eat it year-round! Note that when serving the dish at a group gathering, I put the pecans to the side, just in case someone has a nut allergy. Bon Appetit!

Kale & More Salad

1 10-16 oz. bag kale salad blend or broccoli slaw mix

1 can garbanzo bean   ½ cup dried cranberries

½ cup pecans (optional or on the side)

¾ cup of shredded carrots (if not in the main blend)

1 tsp red pepper flakes   1/3 cup balsamic vinaigrette salad dressing

A pinch of sea salt to taste

Set pecans to the side in a separate bowl. Toss the other ingredients together in a bowl. Add additional red pepper, salt, and salad dressing to taste. Let individuals add in pecans if desired. Quick, healthy, and tasty!

For more quick and healthy dish ideas, go to www.eat2livesociety.com.

<u>Additional Timeout Ideas & Resources</u>

- Get outside! Get grounded! Take off your shoes and socks and soak up some good energy from grass, soil, and/or sand.

- Listen to music.

- Do some gardening.

- Play outside with a family member or friend.

- Solve mazes and word search puzzles.

===

THE 2ND QUARTER PLAYS LESSONS LEARNED 👍☺

Student, list anything that you have realized or learned about yourself, how you work with a team, and your level of focus or commitment. Discuss these lessons with your coach or another teammate and explore how you can improve the situations moving forward.

Date: _____

_____

_____

_____

_____

_____

_____

_____

_____

Date: _____

_____

_____

_____

_____

_____

_____

_____

_____

_____

Date: _____

_____

_____

_____

_____

_____

_____

_____

_____

_____

===

THE 2ND QUARTER WINNING PLAYS {YAY!}

List three to five of your successes over the past one to four weeks! The successes could be in any area of your life. You can also list people, experiences, resources, and things for which you are grateful.

Date: _____

_____

_____

_____

_____

_____

_____

_____

Date: _____

_____

_____

_____

_____

_____

_____

_____

Date: _____

_____

_____

_____

_____

_____

_____

_____

THE 2ND QUARTER SIDELINE NOTES

Coach and Students, write down any next steps to take, adjustments to be made, and any other important information to consider.

Date: _____

_____
_____
_____
_____
_____
_____
_____
_____
_____
_____
_____
_____
_____
_____
_____
_____
_____
_____
_____
_____
_____
_____
_____
_____
_____

THE HALF-TIME LOCKER ROOM CHAT

"You have to believe in yourself when no one else does." ~ Serena Williams

TEST-TAKING & POST-ASSESSMENT PLAYS

Student,

Let's talk about the assessment. Have you taken it yet? If not, please take it. Go to www.themathplaybook.com to get the link and instructions. Get help from your coach to access it if needed.

Once you have taken the assessment and discussed your score with your coach, please rate on a scale of 1 to 10 how you felt when taking the test and your score.

How did you feel when taking the test?

1	2	3	4	5	6	7	8	9	10
Stressed		Nervous		No Feelings		Calm		Confident	

How did you feel once you saw your score?

1	2	3	4	5	6	7	8	9	10
Stressed		Sad		No Feelings		Relieved		Proud	

Talk about these feelings with your coach and team. Review the test-taking tips below, and with your coach, **select two to three strategies** you can put into practice when taking a test in the future. Review those strategies before taking your next test in school or with your team.

TEST-TAKING TIPS

- Become familiar with the test format and how the test will be scored.

- Ensure you have all of the equipment allowed during the test, e. g. a calculator and ruler.

- If allowed, write down any formulas, vocabulary terms definitions, and other information that will help you with the test questions on the test paper or a scratch piece of paper.

- Review the entire test before you start.

- If there is a time limit to complete the test, be mindful of that. Divide the time by the number of questions to determine the average time you should invest when answering each question. Also, try to leave a few minutes to review the test.

- Watch out for extra information not required to simplify or solve a problem, especially a word problem or a data analysis problem. For example, there may be a lot of information in a table, chart, or map. But, only some numbers are needed to provide the correct answer.

- If you are unsure about an answer, skip the question and find another one that you can solve quickly.

- On multiple-choice tests, use the process of elimination. Two of the answers usually make no sense. So, focus on comparing the remaining answer options to isolate the correct one.

- Read each question carefully to ensure you provide or select the answer in the correct form. For example, the question may give fraction values to calculate, but the required answer should be in decimal form.

- You may be able to plug the multiple-choice answer choices into the question or a number sentence to determine which one is the correct solution.

- Lastly, follow up and review the entire test before submitting it to be graded.

Your coach and teammates DO believe in you! Ask one of them to schedule a day and time in the next four to twelve weeks for you to retake the assessment or a similar test. Make sure to consider the study strategies you have decided to implement. Good luck!

Coach,

Use the charts on the next two pages to track your student's improved knowledge and skills of the basic math building blocks. Make sure to celebrate successes and identify rewards for your student's test-taking skills improvement over the next four to twelve weeks. Once your student has mastered the building blocks listed, create another tracking sheet for advanced concepts.

BUILDING BLOCKS STUDY TRACKING SHEET

Number Sense (including Pattern Recognition)   ____ ____ ____ ____

The Four Basic Arithmetic Operations   ____ ____ ____ ____

Multiplication Facts   ____ ____ ____ ____

Prime Numbers   ____ ____ ____ ____

Fractions   ____ ____ ____ ____

Decimals   ____ ____ ____ ____

Percent Values (Percentage)   ____ ____ ____ ____

Data Analysis & Statistics   ____ ____ ____ ____

Integers   ____ ____ ____ ____

Exponents   ____ ____ ____ ____

Order of Operations   ____ ____ ____ ____

Units of Measurement   ____ ____ ____ ____

_____ (e.g., Estimation/Rounding)   ____ ____ ____ ____

_____   ____ ____ ____ ____

33

BUILDING BLOCKS PYRAMID

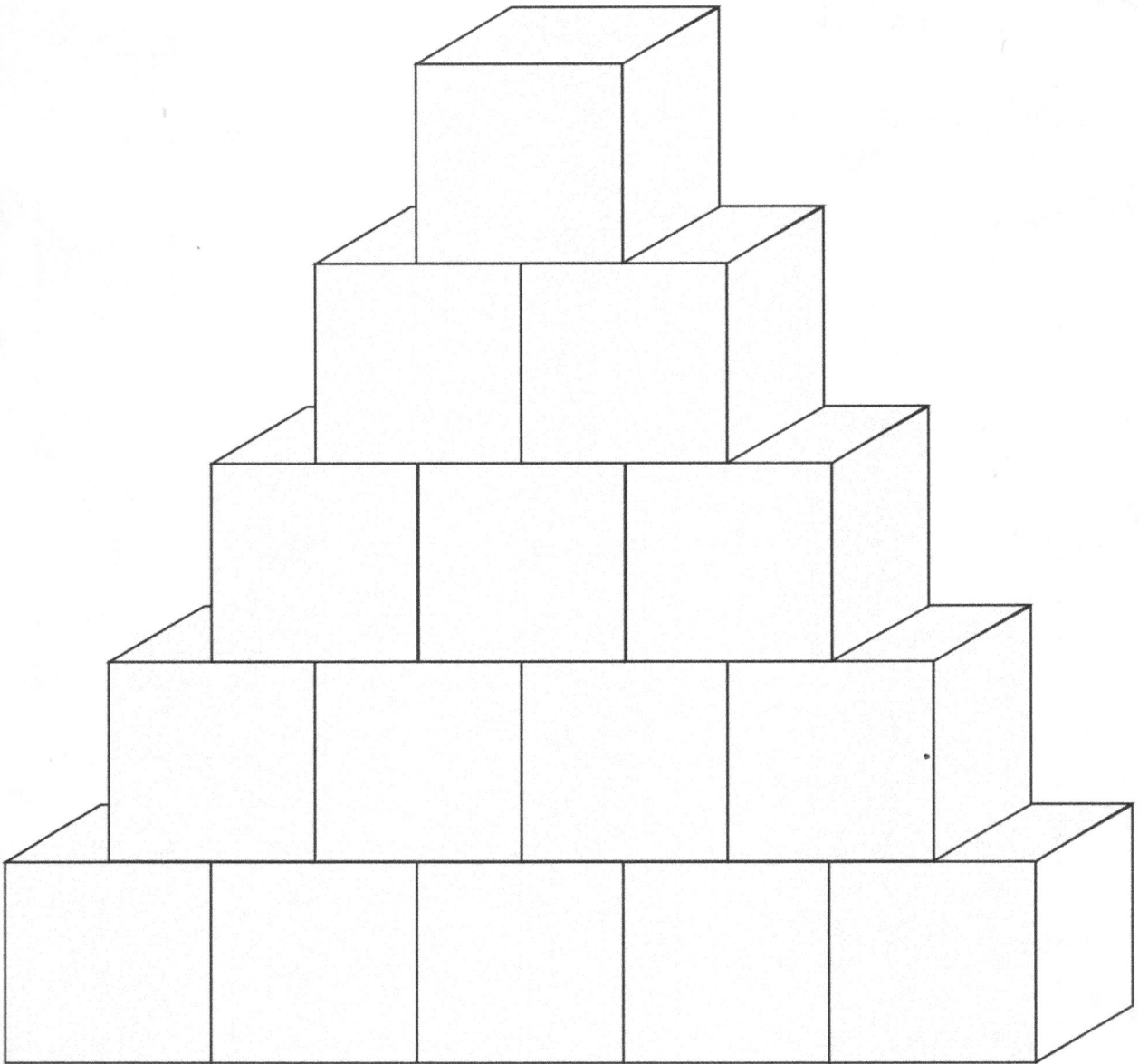

BUILDING BLOCKS STUDY TRACKING SHEET

Study Weeks or Months
(Track the date range.)

_____   ____ ____ ____ ____

_____   ____ ____ ____ ____

_____   ____ ____ ____ ____

_____   ____ ____ ____ ____

_____   ____ ____ ____ ____

_____   ____ ____ ____ ____

_____   ____ ____ ____ ____

_____   ____ ____ ____ ____

_____   ____ ____ ____ ____

_____   ____ ____ ____ ____

_____   ____ ____ ____ ____

_____   ____ ____ ____ ____

_____   ____ ____ ____ ____

THE HALF-TIME REPORT TEAMS UP WITH THE LEARNING STYLES

Coach and Student,

Please review the half-time report in the playbook. Even if your student has not been given an individualized education or 504 plan, there may be accommodations discussed that will enhance your student's learning, understanding, application, and mastery of the basic math concepts/building blocks.

Afterward, if you have not done so yet, review the learning styles in The 1st Quarter of the playbook and revisit your answer to the learning styles question on page 4 of this book. Student, based on your strongest or primary learning style, identify which of the basic accommodations may improve your math game. Also, consider the accommodations that may strengthen the other learning modes for you since the goal is to be a well-rounded learner by using a combination of all of the learning styles.

LOCKER ROOM – MATH MENTAL ENRICHMENT ACTIVITIES

Coach and Student,

If you have not already done so, plan and calendar a family (and friends) game night or other group activities that include scorekeeping. Turn off the television and put away everyone's phones, except to take photos. Yes, make it memorable! Make it fun!

==

HALF-TIME LOCKER ROOM CHAT 👉☺

Student,

    List anything that you have learned about yourself, your test-taking skills, your basic math building blocks knowledge, and/or your study strategies during half-time. Discuss these lessons and how you can improve the situations moving forward with your coach or another teammate.

_____

_____

_____

_____

_____

_____

_____

_____

_____

_____

_____

_____

_____

_____

_____

_____

_____

_____

==

HALF-TIME LOCKER ROOM NOTES

THE 3rd QUARTER PLAYS

"You can't put a limit on anything. The more you dream, the farther you get."
~ Michael Phelps

==

YOUR WHY?

Student, if you know your Why?/Chief Aim/Ultimate Life Path Goal, which is often phrased as "What do you want to be when you grow up?", then great; you have a goal in mind, so it should be easier to set short-term goals and plans to keep you on the path to your Why?/Chief Aim. Whether you do or don't, list your favorite school subjects, hobbies… to help you determine or refine your long-term goals. Also, list **why** they are your favorites.

- School Subjects

  _____
  _____
  _____

- Hobbies

  _____
  _____
  _____

- TV Shows

  _____
  _____
  _____

-
  Music

  _____
  _____
  _____

- Movies

  _____
  _____
  _____

- Sports

  _____
  _____
  _____

- Dream Vacation

  _____
  _____
  _____

- Service to Community

  _____
  _____
  _____

==

Career Assessment

Student,

Access the interests/career assessment below. Once you complete and score it, share the results with your coach.

- Do the results reveal any surprises?

  _____
  _____
  _____

- Do the results confirm your WHY??

  _____
  _____
  _____

- Do the results suggest you have current hobbies and interests that are related to the interests/careers results identified?

  _____
  _____
  _____

Make sure to discuss the results and your insights with your team.

Take this assessment (or a similar one) every six months to confirm or make adjustments to your WHY?. Be mindful that we can have numerous interests, like a track and field athlete may participate in various events. We are living longer and have global access to lots of information and opportunities. So be open to any changes in your dreams, goals, interests, and long-term WHY?.

https://tinyurl.com/TMPcareerinv

"We are all purposed for success."
~Ruby Leah

PUT YOUR PLAN ON PAPER

Student,

Work with your coach to put your plan on paper. Be honest with your coach and team about your ideal study times, ideal study locations, and any additional equipment or resources you need to stick to the agreed-upon schedules. Use the monthly calendar and the weekly schedule sheet in the playbook appendices or other scheduling materials to put your commitment in writing. Post the schedules in your study area and in a location that the entire team can access. Take photos of the schedules and keep them posted on your digital devices. Add events and reminders to your digital devices for access on the go. Keep these student's takeaways from the related sections in *The Math Playbook* in mind when creating, scheduling, and implementing your winning game plan.

- Consider your WHY?.
- Become aware of what motivates and inspires you to take action. Your goals, learning style, on-hand equipment, teamwork efforts, learning environment, energy, and personality type are all important factors to consider.
- Make a list of enrichment activities you already enjoy.

_____
_____
_____

- Confirm the building blocks to study with your coach or another teammate.
- Review the math-mental tips, tricks, and time-saving strategies in The 3rd Quarter of the playbook with your coach, a tutor, or another teammate.
- Study or review the arithmetic properties.
- Study or review class notes daily.
- Have fun!

GOALS

==

REAL-LIFE PLAYS

Stay in the zone! Math is everywhere! Over the next week or two, list three to five daily experiences or activities where you've seen math in action. Examples include shopping, cooking, watching a sporting event, riding in a car, and enrichment activities. Write down the experiences and activities and how math was involved. Also, discuss your observations with your coach or teammates.

Date: _____

_____

_____

_____

Date: _____

_____

_____

_____

Date: _____

_____

_____

_____

Date: _____

_____

_____

_____

Date: _____

_____

_____

_____

WIN!

==

==

PRACTICE, CONDITIONING, & DRILLS

Student, it's that time again! Practice, practice, and more practice with conditioning and drills are a must! Please review the vocabulary list below and the multiplication facts list on an upcoming page. Talk with your coach to determine which one you want to tackle next – vocabulary terms or multiplication facts. The vocabulary list is shared again for your convenience. But, I recommend you copy it and add it to your activities binder and post it on the refrigerator or another highly visible location.

You know the drill. ☺ Select five to ten vocabulary terms and one to two multiplication facts sets to learn, understand, and/or memorize over the next 7 to 14 days using the Vocabulary Mastery Activities on the next page. The multiplication activities are again provided in an upcoming section. If you don't see vocabulary terms that you need to master, use your math book or other resources to learn terms that you will be using in upcoming lessons or classes.

Again, use the study techniques on the following pages to guide your efforts. Ask your coach or a teammate to help you set up these activities if needed.

Arithmetic/Applied Arithmetic/Pre-Algebra Vocabulary

real number   absolute value   counting numbers   odd number
 even number   prime number   composite number   whole number
number line   integer   positive number   negative number
rational number   irrational number   ascending order   descending order
****
place value   ones   units   tens   hundreds-thousands
ten-thousands   digit   round   estimate   approximate(ly)
****
add   plus   together   sum   total   increase   addend
****
subtract   minus   takeaway   difference   fewer than   less than   decrease
          reduce   reduction   deduction
****
multiply   times   factor (n)   product   double

==

twice   triple quadruple   of   exponent   power   order of operation

****

divide   divisor   dividend   quotient   factor (v)   separate
into   equal   parts   inverse   operation   reciprocal

****

decimal   decimal point   digit   tenth
hundredth   thousandth   ten-thousandth

****

fraction   numerator   denominator   improper fraction   mixed number
reciprocal   multiplicative inverse   ratio   proportion

****

percent   part   whole   of   is   total

****

unknown   variable   constant   order of operation

****

problem   exercise   Equation   expression   sentence
solve   simplify   calculate   compute   evaluate
equal   equivalent same as   average   mean
median   mode   range   greater than   less than
greater than or equal   less than or equal   compare   graph

****

linear   one-dimensional   two-dimensional   three-dimensional

<u>Vocabulary Mastery Activities</u>

Coach and Student,

I am sharing this information again for your convenience. Dedicate 15 to 30 minutes to the activities 2 to 5 days a week for the next 7 to 14 days. Determine a convenient time when you can focus on completing the activities. Post those times on a calendar and/or planner. Use the weekly schedule in the playbook appendices.

Coach,

On Day 1, you (or a teammate) can give your student a written assessment on 10 to 15 terms from the list at a time. Use your student's math book or other resources to obtain the definitions and applications of the math vocabulary if needed. With the assessment results, assign your student 5 to 10 terms to study over a one-week to two-week span. Create a list of the terms on a piece of paper and post them on the refrigerator to view daily. Encourage family members to reference this list to help your student learn, understand, and apply the terms.

Student,

Commit to the 15 to 30 minutes time slot selected. Find a comfortable place to do these activities – comfortable seating and adequate lighting. Have snacks and study tools on hand. Turn on background music if it helps you focus.

DAY 0

    1. Take the assessment. To the best of your ability, write the definition of each term **in your own words**.

    2. Have your coach or another team member correct your answers.

DAY 1

    For any term that you don't know yet, write the term with the correct definition THREE times each in your math journal or a binder. Use your math textbook or go to www.mathsisfun.com/basic-math-definitions.html or other resources to get more understanding of these terms.

BONUS ACTIVITY – *Use a recording device to create an auditory fill-in-the-blank exercise to practice. Record yourself. First, state the definition of a term. Pause for three to five seconds. Then say the term. Leave the silent space between stating each definition and its correct term. Do this for each term on your list.* **The silent space will allow time you to later say the term before the answer is revealed on the recording.** *(This activity can be done outside of study time and is a great activity for auditory learners!)*

DAY 2

Create and use flashcards to study the terms.

DAY 3

Write the terms and definitions one to three times each.

DAY 4

1. Use the flashcards or the bonus activity to study/test yourself on the terms and definitions.

2. OR, define the terms and explain them to your coach or another team member. If you get 80% of the answers correct – CONGRATULATIONS!!!!!

DAY 5

Ask your coach or another team member to give you a written post-assessment. Take note of any incorrect answers and write those terms and definitions three times each. If you get 80% or more of the answers correct – CONGRATULATIONS!!!!!

Repeat this activity up to three times with new sets of five to ten words before moving on to The 4ᵗʰ Quarter Plays activities. Coach, set up the next week's/section's practice set to include two or three of the terms from the previous week(s), especially those that your student hasn't mastered yet, for review and reinforcement.

==

<u>Multiplications Facts Families</u>

Student,

Pick up where you left off in The 1st Quarter Plays multiplication facts activities. Use the practice sheets that are available on www.math-drils.com, www.math-aids.com, www.purplemath.com, or from other resources to which you have access to give yourself practice drills.

Continue to study and memorize the facts in the order shown below. Please use this strategy and the tracking sheet you printed out (or copy it from The 1st Quarter now). Get help from your coach or a teammate if needed.

0, 1, 2, 5, 10, 11, 9, 3, 4, 6, 7, 8, 12

Reminder, through my experience with students on various grade levels, this order allows students to learn more information at a faster rate by using tips, tricks, and time-saving strategies like patterns that are more obvious in certain factor families. For example, the multiplication facts for the number nine (9) are easy to remember because the digits of the products add up to 9 – 9 x 3 = 27……. 2 + 7 = 9.

If you already know the facts sets for numbers 1 to 12, then learn the facts for 13-16, 20, and 25.

Reminder: Put the completed activity sheets in your math journal/binder or multiplication facts activities binder.

==

FUN & GAMES – MATH-MENTAL ENRICHMENT ACTIVITIES

Student, it is important to make learning fun! If you ever feel overwhelmed or lose focus when studying math concepts at home, call "Timeout!" Let your coach know you need to take a 15 to 30 minute mental break. Get some fresh air, turn on some music, move your body, create some art, play a game, and/or engage in an enrichment activity (Choose a game or activity that is not on television or on an electronic device.☺)

Here is a puzzle to solve when you need to take a break. Have fun!

BASIC MATH TERMS

For the answers, go to www.themathplaybook.com.

Y	D	E	M	M	T	Y	X	B	K	O	O	S	P	V	G	L	O
X	G	L	T	Y	X	O	Q	B	E	N	U	D	T	J	R	U	J
Q	U	O	T	I	E	N	T	T	O	E	G	E	C	A	O	Y	R
D	E	A	D	D	I	T	I	O	N	S	W	R	U	H	T	Y	U
X	I	W	N	A	D	D	E	N	D	R	L	D	D	E	A	Q	Z
Q	F	V	O	W	T	E	W	P	B	P	O	N	O	K	N	H	Z
O	C	R	I	R	A	I	U	I	T	T	J	U	R	A	I	Z	N
S	Y	A	T	S	B	W	F	X	N	O	V	H	P	T	M	P	M
U	Z	J	A	D	I	F	F	E	R	E	N	C	E	K	O	O	L
B	K	X	C	C	Q	O	C	L	Z	T	Y	G	V	R	N	I	A
T	E	A	I	L	V	R	N	V	Q	E	X	F	O	V	E	T	M
R	V	U	L	Q	E	X	P	Z	T	N	I	T	A	M	D	A	I
A	S	D	P	P	V	N	E	R	Q	S	A	Y	K	C	L	R	C
C	R	S	I	T	P	Z	O	S	F	R	W	W	U	C	T	T	E
T	E	U	T	V	T	Q	F	T	E	N	V	X	I	H	Z	O	D
I	G	M	L	V	L	H	Z	M	I	U	X	L	F	G	C	G	R
O	U	C	U	E	K	C	U	W	F	R	A	C	T	I	O	N	O
N	K	Z	M	Z	Z	N	T	O	M	X	E	Q	U	A	L	K	O

Addition	Equal	Sum
Subtraction	Ratio	Difference
Multiplication	Ones	Product
Division	Tens	Factor
Fraction	Hundreds	Quotient
Decimal	Numerator	
Percent	Denominator	

<u>Additional Timeout Ideas & Resources</u>

- Read a jokes book (that you have checked out from the library).

- Take a walk with a family member or friend.

- Draw, doodle, or paint.

- Play a card came.

- Play a musical instrument.

THE 3RD QUARTER PLAYS LESSONS LEARNED 👍

Student, list anything that you have realized or learned about your favorite things/activities, WHY?, and your math study strategies plan up until now. Discuss these lessons with your coach or another teammate and explore how you can improve the situations moving forward.

Date: _____

_____
_____
_____
_____
_____
_____
_____

Date: _____

_____
_____
_____
_____
_____
_____
_____
_____
_____

Date: _____

_____
_____
_____
_____
_____
_____
_____
_____
_____

==

THE 3RD QUARTER WINNING PLAYS (YAY!)

List three to five of your successes over the past one to four weeks! The successes could be in any area of your life. You can also list people, experiences, resources, and things for which you are grateful.

Date: _____

_____

_____

_____

_____

_____

_____

_____

Date: _____

_____

_____

_____

_____

_____

_____

_____

Date: _____

_____

_____

_____

_____

_____

_____

_____

==

THE 3RD QUARTER SIDELINE NOTES

Coach and Student, write down any next steps to take, adjustments to be made, and any other important information to consider.

Date: _____

_____

_____

_____

_____

_____

_____

_____

_____

_____

_____

_____

_____

_____

_____

_____

_____

_____

_____

_____

_____

_____

_____

_____

_____

_____

THE 4th QUARTER PLAYS

"You have to fight for your dream. You have to sacrifice and work hard for it."
~Lionel Messi

Coach and Student,

It's time to do some math! Focus on the 12 foundational building blocks covered in *The Math Playbook* and additional building blocks/math concepts depending on your current grade level or math class. Copy the building blocks tracking sheet set. Two sets have been provided. Keep one set as a master to copy, as your student will be using these tracking sheets for the rest of his or her math-learning journey.

BUILDING BLOCKS TRACKING & PLAYS STRATEGIES SHEETS

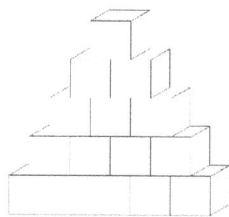

Coach and Student,

These tracking sheets are to serve as activities initially and then as references and resources. So, make sure to keep them in a binder for long-term access. Begin filling out two to four over the next one to three weeks as a part of The 4th Quarter Plays. Again, make sure to make copies of the blank pages to utilize the sheets for long-term learning. Add them to your activity binder, and journal binder, and/or create a binder for each building block/math concept. Add information to each sheet as you move through your (student's) math curriculum and notice real-life experiences that apply. Create as many pages as needed for each building block. This set-up activity will serve your team in the current math class and in the future.

Student,

You may choose to begin with the building blocks that you are currently studying in school or another formal academic setting. You can also begin with those foundational building blocks that are "stumbling blocks" for you, up until now, based on the assessment you completed in the playbook resources. Starting on the sheet on page 59, list the name of the building block or advanced math concept on the blank line. As you study each new building block, create a set of pages for it. Write down the associated.

- Vocabulary terms
- Rules of operations
- Examples of the computations
- How and where the math concept is applied in other math concepts, other academic subjects, and/or real-life settings
- Visual/graphic representation
- Connections to other building blocks/math concepts
- Connections to algebra, geometry, and statistics concepts
- Connections to other concepts in other academic subjects

- Connections to real-life situations
- Websites, apps, and other resources to enrich learning and understanding of the building block/math concept

Use colored pencils, markers, and post it notes to improve the effectiveness of these building block game strategy tracking sheets. Once you advance beyond the arithmetic and applied arithmetic building blocks that are discussed or mentioned in *The Math Playbook*; create sheets for other concepts, including those encountered in pre-algebra, algebra, statistics, geometry, physics, chemistry, and other math-based coursework.

_____ BUILDING BLOCK TRACKING & PLAYS STRATEGIES SHEET

Grade(s)/Class(es) _____

Date(s): _____

Reminder, add to this sheet over time – days, weeks, or longer. Once it is completed, add it to your binder.

Key Vocabulary Terms (with definitions)

_____
_____
_____
_____
_____
_____
_____
_____
_____

Rules of Operations (addition, subtraction, multiplication, division, exponents and others)

_____
_____
_____
_____
_____
_____
_____
_____
_____
_____

Exercise Examples

_____
_____
_____
_____
_____
_____

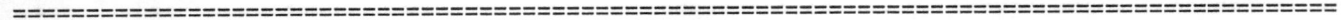

Grade(s)/Class(es): _____
Date(s): _____

Applications – How, when, and/or why is this building block/concept used in mathematics and in real-life situations?

_____

_____

_____

_____

_____

_____

_____

_____

Visual/Graphic Representation of this building block (drawings, graphs, and other visual images that reinforce learning, understanding, and application to move you toward mastery)

Grade(s)/Class(es): _____
Date(s): _____

Connections to other Building Blocks

_____
_____
_____
_____
_____
_____
_____
_____
_____
_____

Connections to Algebra and/or Geometry

_____
_____
_____
_____
_____
_____
_____
_____
_____
_____

Connections to other Academic Subjects

_____
_____
_____
_____
_____
_____
_____
_____
_____
_____

Grade(s)/Class(es) _____

Date(s): _____

Real-life Connections

_____
_____
_____
_____
_____
_____
_____
_____
_____
_____

Resources

_____
_____
_____
_____
_____
_____
_____
_____
_____

Notes

_____
_____
_____
_____
_____
_____

_____ BUILDING BLOCK TRACKING & PLAYS STRATEGIES SHEET

Grade(s)/Class(es) _____

Date(s): _____

Reminder, add to this sheet over time – days, weeks, or longer. Once it is completed, add it to your binder.

Key Vocabulary Terms (with definitions)

_____

_____

_____

_____

_____

_____

_____

_____

_____

_____

Rules of Operations (addition, subtraction, multiplication, division, exponents and others)

_____

_____

_____

_____

_____

_____

_____

_____

_____

_____

Exercise Examples

_____

_____

_____

_____

_____

_____

Grade(s)/Class(es): _____
Date(s): _____

Applications – How, when, and/or why is this building block/concept used in mathematics and in real-life situations?

_____
_____
_____
_____
_____
_____
_____
_____

Visual/Graphic Representation of this building block (drawings, graphs, and other visual images that reinforce learning, understanding, and application to move you toward mastery)

Grade(s)/Class(es): _____

Date(s): _____

Connections to other Building Blocks

_____

_____

_____

_____

_____

_____

_____

_____

_____

_____

Connections to Algebra and/or Geometry

_____

_____

_____

_____

_____

_____

_____

_____

_____

_____

Connections to other Academic Subjects

_____

_____

_____

_____

_____

_____

_____

_____

_____

_____

Grade(s)/Class(es) _____
Date(s): _____

Real-life Connections

_____
_____
_____
_____
_____
_____
_____
_____

Resources

_____
_____
_____
_____
_____
_____
_____
_____

Notes

_____
_____
_____
_____
_____
_____

FUN & GAMES – MATH MENTAL ENRICHMENT ACTIVITIES

Student, remember to make learning fun! As you continue to move through the building blocks and other math concepts, give yourself a mental break as needed. When you feel overwhelmed or lose focus, call "Timeout!" Let your coach know you need to take a 15 to 30 minute mental break. Get some fresh air, turn on some music, move your body, create some art, play a game, and/or engage in an enrichment activity (Choose a game or activity that is not on television or on an electronic device.☺)

Here is a puzzle to solve when you need to take a break. Have fun!

SPORTS

For the answers, go to www.themathplaybook.com.

Y	C	C	Y	C	L	I	N	G	K	O	U	I	G	V	H	R	Z
L	A	P	G	N	I	C	N	E	F	N	J	G	F	F	R	D	I
D	N	C	G	N	I	T	F	I	L	T	H	G	I	E	W	Z	D
O	J	U	B	S	C	I	T	S	A	N	M	Y	G	J	P	H	U
R	M	A	R	A	T	H	O	N	A	R	N	I	W	M	A	K	T
T	V	P	Y	U	S	G	L	R	P	G	N	I	I	K	S	Y	B
H	L	K	P	T	Z	K	C	W	L	V	E	S	M	M	H	K	A
D	F	X	W	W	E	H	E	Y	J	T	Q	T	P	J	R	G	S
N	B	I	H	X	E	N	E	T	L	H	R	A	C	I	N	G	E
G	W	W	K	R	B	L	N	S	B	Q	W	B	H	I	H	Y	B
N	R	G	Y	L	L	L	R	I	L	A	S	X	M	K	P	Q	A
I	E	G	O	O	U	A	E	R	S	A	L	M	P	E	Y	T	L
F	S	N	W	K	O	B	C	H	V	C	I	L	H	V	W	E	L
R	T	I	F	C	I	T	C	L	I	W	U	J	X	G	B	I	L
U	L	T	X	I	N	O	O	W	S	T	B	T	B	F	L	O	G
S	I	A	C	L	Y	O	S	H	L	X	K	Y	Q	I	E	X	A
F	N	K	J	O	G	F	D	V	O	L	L	E	Y	B	A	L	L
L	G	S	W	Q	R	Y	X	L	Y	B	G	U	R	L	M	F	U

Football	Gymnastics	Archery
Basketball	Wrestling	Skiing
Tennis	Skating	Racing
Golf	Surfing	Baseball
Soccer	Volleyball	Marathon
Swimming	Rugby	Weightlifting
Fencing		Cycling

<u>Additional Timeout Ideas & Resources</u>

- Plan a fun activity to do with family and friends.

- Read a funny book or magazine.

- Make a snack.

- Make a grocery list.

- Stretch.

THE 4ᵀᴴ QUARTER PLAYS LESSONS LEARNED 👆

Student, list anything that you have realized or learned about yourself and your understanding of the math building blocks up until now. Discuss these lessons with your coach or another teammate and explore how you can improve the situations moving forward.

Date: _____

_____
_____
_____
_____
_____
_____
_____
_____

Date: _____

_____
_____
_____
_____
_____
_____
_____
_____
_____

Date: _____

_____
_____
_____
_____
_____
_____
_____
_____
_____

THE 4TH QUARTER WINNING PLAYS (YAY!)

List three to five of your successes over the past one to four weeks! Consider successes related to your learning, understanding, applying, and/or mastering any of the building blocks. You can also list people, experiences, resources, and things for which you are grateful.

Date: _____

_____

_____

_____

_____

_____

_____

_____

Date: _____

_____

_____

_____

_____

_____

_____

_____

Date: _____

_____

_____

_____

_____

_____

_____

_____

THE 4ᵀᴴ QUARTER SIDELINE NOTES

Coach and Student, now that you have worked with some of the building blocks strategies, write down any next steps to take, adjustments to be made, and any other important information to consider.

Date: _____

_____
_____
_____
_____
_____
_____
_____
_____
_____
_____
_____
_____
_____
_____
_____
_____
_____
_____
_____
_____
_____
_____
_____
_____
_____
_____

==

STAY COMMITTED

"Take those chances and you can achieve greatness, whereas if you go conservative, you'll never know." ~ Danica Patrick

Coach and Student,

Now that you are at the two-minute warning let's revisit your level of commitment. Like the athletes who are quoted in this book, your team must stay focused and stay in the zone. Review and update your commitment sheets.

Student,

What is a game, activity, project, or cause that you have been committed to until completion? What inspired you to stay with it? How did you feel once it was completed? Let that feeling set you up for future games and future wins.

_____

_____

_____

What are three to five actions you can take to stay committed even when obstacles appear? Discuss this with your coach. Keep these strategies posted in your study area or on the refrigerator.

_____

_____

_____

What are three easy short-term goals (over the next 30 days) that you are committed to achieving?

_____

_____

_____

What are three ways in which you can make the above actions needed to attain the goals easy and fun?

_____

_____

_____

have fun

==

IT'S A LIFELONG GAME!

"Don't count the days; make the days count." ~ Muhammad Ali

Congratulations on completing this season of the game of math! I hope you took my advice and made copies of the pages for the next game season (grade level or class) and future seasons! Again, Coach and Student, use the content of this workbook with all of the activity entries that you completed as reference and resource material. Continue the building blocks tracking activities. Review and refresh the information consistently to execute more winning plays inside and outside the classroom! Remember to review what worked and did not work for your team during this season in the Coach's Corner sections of *The Math Playbook* and in a math journal, so you can determine your game plan for the next season – school year or class!

God's continued blessings and success inside and outside the game of math!

Sincerely,

Teresa

www.ingramcontent.com/pod-product-compliance
Lightning Source LLC
Chambersburg PA
CBHW062053090426

42740CB00016B/3125